GOOD GUYS

GOOD GUYS

THE EIGHT STEPS TO LIMITLESS POSSIBILITY FOR FRATERNITY RECRUITMENT

MATTHEW G. MATTSON
JOSHUA A. ORENDI

A Product of Phired Up Productions, LLC

Created and published by

Phired Up Productions, LLC

727 Genesee Dr.

Naperville, IL 60563

Matthew G. Mattson and Joshua A. Orendi

Good Guys: The Eight Steps to Limitless Possibility for

Fraternity Recruitment / Mattson & Orendi

Printed in the United States of America

First Edition

http://www.PhiredUp.com

This book is dedicated to

Louis Manigault, Founder of ΑΣΦ

He's the guy, who recruited the guy, who recruited the guy, who

recruited the guy, who recruited the guy…

…who recruited us.

Special thanks to:

Rick Deale	Christopher Boniface
Ed Lenane	Kyle Jordan
Heath Stephens	Mike Post
Matt Maurer	Tom Hinkley
Colleen Coffey	Drew Thawley
Kristi Hoffman	Sandra Moore, Editor

Alpha Sigma Phi Fraternity, Inc

…and most importantly, our wives

Meggan Mattson

Denise Orendi

Your house may have different letters on it than mine, but our foundations are built from the same stone.

TABLE OF CONTENTS

DO IT.

Throughout *Good Guys* you will find practical applications to help you improve your recruitment results immediately. Pay special attention to the sections entitled **"Do It."** These sections provide exercises and activities to help you get immediate results.

FOREWORD: LESSONS LEARNED   **7**

THE BEST GUYS ON CAMPUS   **13**

    DO IT.   18

THE EIGHT STEPS TO LIMITLESS...   **19**

THE STAGE IS SET   **23**

STEP 1: KNOW THE BASICS   **27**

    DO IT.   31

STEP 2: A.C.E. YOUR VALUES   **35**

    DO IT.   48

S.P.A.M.   **49**

STEP 3: GET MOTIVATED   **59**
DO IT.   70

STEP 4: KNOW YOUR AUDIENCE   **73**
DO IT.   92

STEP 5: KNOW YOUR PRODUCT   **95**
DO IT.   104

STEP 6: DEVELOP SKILLS   **107**
DO IT.   128

STEP 7: GROW WISER   **131**
DO IT.   140

STEP 8: REPEAT   **143**
DO IT.   150

WHO DOES ALL THIS?   **151**

THE EIGHT STEPS IN REVIEW   **153**

FREQUENTLY ASKED QUESTIONS   **157**

DO IT.   **159**

FOREWORD: LESSONS LEARNED

This book is about recruiting gentlemen into college fraternities (though you'll find the messages to be universally applicable). We believe recruitment is at the core of a fraternity's potential and at the core of most fraternities' major challenges.

That being said, you should know that we (the authors, Matt and Josh) used to be really bad at recruitment. We're talking bad. Not like when "bad" really meant good, but actually bad.

When we were undergraduate fraternity men we both dreaded that "rush" time of the year. We didn't like that we felt fake and cheesy when just trying to get a few strangers to join our chapter within the allotted rush week. Because we didn't like it, we never learned anything about it, and we didn't get any better at it while we were in college.

Then, while working at our fraternity's national headquarters (Alpha Sigma Phi) as Chapter Leadership Consultants, we decided to apply for a promotion to share the role of Director of Expansion. That essentially meant that we would be *the* brothers in charge of recruitment for the entire national organization. The future growth of a 150-year-old organization with tens of thousands of living brothers would be solely in our hands.

Somehow we got the job and, honestly, we were still really bad at recruitment. We tried some expansion efforts at a few universities along the East Coast; and while most of them ultimately "succeeded," our success was mostly due to the dedication of the few undergraduate leaders at those schools.

Anyway, to make a long story short, we left our posts as Directors of Expansion after a while; we had some work and life experiences in which we were forced to learn how to do sales, recruitment, and relationship building; we read some books; we got involved in other organizations; and we got a LOT better at recruitment. We studied the best recruiters, fraternity men, salespeople, managers and leaders in the field, and we quickly realized that it would have been really helpful had we had this information, knowledge and wisdom while we were in college.

In 2002, we founded Phired Up Productions, LLC as a way to get the message out about membership growth and development for non-profit organizations – especially college fraternities. Nobody had ever taught us how to do any of this while we were in college, and we became determined to change that for others. We hadn't learned it in classes, we hadn't learned it in our new member education programs, and we had definitely never read any books about it when we were in school.

Nobody teaches you this stuff!

Yada, yada, yada… Now we're writing a book about how to discover limitless possibilities for your fraternity, all of which is based on the premise that if you had a system to recruit a higher quantity of higher quality members, you would have more money as a chapter, you would have more friends as a chapter, and you could do more fun things as a chapter. Essentially, a better amount of better people makes a better organization.

Good news! You don't have to wait until you're old like us to discover the limitless possibilities of your fraternity experience. And, if by chance you're reading this after your storied undergraduate years have passed, don't worry. You can do a lot to make the future of our struggling but proud fraternity community as bright as possible by advocating and practicing the eight step model found in this book.

Someone a lot smarter than us once said, "The two ways people learn are by making mistakes and taking note of the mistakes made by others." We hope the lessons of our failures speed your successes.

The paradigm of fraternity recruitment is about to experience a revolution. The model in this book, if it is learned, shared, and practiced, provides the framework for that revolution of limitless possibilities.

May you see your potential, may you work hard, and may your dreams be achieved!

"Associate yourself with men of good quality if you esteem your reputation. It is better to be alone than in bad company."

~George Washington~

THE BEST GUYS ON CAMPUS

After hours of heated debate, the color and design of this year's rush T-shirts are determined. The T-shirts arrive just in time for the big week. At the last minute the chapter throws together several events for IFC (Interfraternity Council) rush week. A few members print up fliers and chalk the sidewalks of campus. One brother leverages his artistic ability to produce a large rush banner on a white bed sheet.

The chapter invests most of its available funds and hundreds of man hours into preparing for the arrival of freshmen prospects. The IFC events are OK, but the real recruiting happens at the chapter's Big Event. They're known for Big Event and have a lot of pride in this special occasion.

Nobody is quite sure who will be coming to Big Event, but everyone is sure it will be Big. Prospective members will be asking for bids by the dozens when they see how the chapter can make Big Event come together. Special care has been given to cleaning the house (sort of), the women have been invited, beverages are provided, and free food is available. The chapter is now prepared for the best rush ever.

Big Event goes relatively well since everyone had a good time. However, the brothers ate most of the free food, the girls in attendance were mostly the brothers' current girlfriends, and nobody seems to remember but a handful of the prospects by name – except for the 2-3 guys everyone sort of knew were going to pledge regardless.

With the lessons of Big Event learned, the chapter realizes it needs to "step it up" since the rush period is half over. So they regroup and have… another Big Event.

As rush week comes to a close, the brothers huddle in a room together to begin the infamous voting process. A few guys slide through with a unanimous "yes." Then, a brother slouched on a couch at the back of the room questions a prospect's credibility and someone else yells out, "Yeah, I don't even know the kid." Another says, "That's what the pledge period is for." Finally, a brother calmly says, "Trust me, he's a good guy." A few others chime in, "Yeah, give him a chance. He seems like a good guy to me." With that, the criteria has been set and the chapter is now several hours deep in a hot room to determine who is "good guy" enough to receive a bid.

Most of the small percentage of freshmen they've met are given bids, but only half of those bids are accepted. The chapter is shocked! However, the brothers set things at ease by reminding themselves that – just like last semester – they got "the best guys on campus."

"Besides," they say, "we're about quality, not quantity."

Did anything sound familiar in that story?

If you can relate even a little, we're laughing right along with you. It's OK, you're involved with a chapter stuck in a traditional recruitment process that we call *Static Recruitment*.

If you can't completely relate to that story, congratulations! You're probably involved in a new chapter or, just maybe, you're fortunate enough to be in the tiny upper echelon of college fraternity chapters today that practice *Dynamic Recruitment*. Dynamic Recruitment is the year round proactive process of seeking high quality men through a system built for success.

This book is for you no matter if that story was exactly like your reality or far from it. *Good Guys* is a book meant to take your chapter from good to great, from static to dynamic, or even from dynamic to unbelievable.

We've found out from our experience gained working with fraternities at all types of schools – big, small, private, public, urban, rural, etc. – that there are a few commonalities that might have hit home for you in that story.

1. Fraternities have some traditions that could be changed. A lot
    of fraternities keep doing the same old things and keep
    getting the same old results.

2. Many fraternities have a disease: *Eventitis*. Eventitis is a
    nasty disease that makes all those chapters infected believe
    they have to spend a lot of money and time on planning a big
    event in order to make friends.

3. No matter how incredible your rush events are, not many
    people come (because most non-fraternity people are scared
    of fraternity events), and if they do happen to come,
    NOBODY EVER JOINS SPECIFICALLY BECAUSE OF
    YOUR COOL EVENT!

4. The truth about rush is that the chapter on campus who gets
    the most strangers to pledge is considered the *winner*. This is
    the epitome of old school Static Recruitment.

     Our story about a typical rush period may not apply to
you and your chapter with 100% accuracy. Your chapter
probably falls somewhere on a continuum of the difference
between a fraternity chapter that practices Static Recruitment and

a fraternity chapter committed to the ideas in this book, the practice of Dynamic Recruitment.

Whether you realize it, your current recruitment process is good. We know this because it was good enough to get you, and we're excited that you've decided to make it great.

Each reader of this book has different needs. Some are desperate for recruitment help because their chapter's immediate survival depends on it. If that's you, we suggest you take the contents of this book pretty seriously. Some readers might be happy with their current recruitment system. If that's you, we recommend that you look for a couple of ideas in this book to help you become even better. We are confident that every fraternity chapter needs some aspect of this book.

A quality fraternity is the most under-appreciated asset on any college campus today. There is no other opportunity for young men that offers the breadth and depth of real-life learning and leadership opportunities than the fraternity experience does. We believe in the idea of fraternity, and we believe that a revolution can begin right now – with you – to take the college fraternity movement into the world of limitless possibilities.

DO IT.

Experience the limitless possibilities that await your chapter right away by applying the ideas provided here:

* **Share the Static Recruitment story with your brothers and see which parts they identify with. Use this to lead a conversation about implementing the changes in this book.**

* **Ask the most involved leaders in the chapter about the moment they knew they were going to join and the person who most influenced their decision. This insight provides wisdom into more effective ways to attract top talent.**

* **Think about the men who never really got involved the way you hoped or who quit the organization early on. Why did they join, who influenced their decision, and what lessons can you learn from their departure to improve your recruitment and retention efforts?**

* **Ask yourself and your fellow chapter brothers which recruitment efforts *actually* get results. What *actually* works to get quality men into your organization?**

The Eight Steps to Limitless Possibility

We share a bond. You understand, just like we do, that our lifelong commitment to fraternal values is rooted in the virtue of humanity. All that is good in the world is represented in fraternity men – sometimes anyway. You also understand, like we do, that sometimes it can be downright hard to convince others of your fraternity's value; getting them to join you in a lifelong friendship can be even more difficult.

Every brother in your organization has sworn the same oath, pledging a life-long commitment to your founding principles and the perpetuation of your brotherhood. The actualization of your collective commitment to living and growing the organization determines your success as a fraternity. In practice, that means growing the *quantity and quality* of your brothers.

The systematic approach presented in this book is a program for maximizing your potential as a world-class fraternity chapter. The Eight Steps to Limitless Possibility is often thought of as just a recruitment model but, if you look closely, you'll see that it is much more than that. It is a system that builds healthy,

self-sustaining, values-based organizations that achieve
unimaginable success.

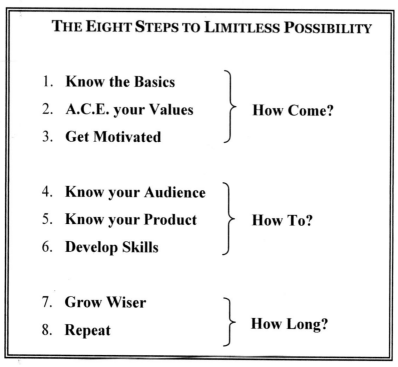

THE EIGHT STEPS TO LIMITLESS POSSIBILITY

1. **Know the Basics**
2. **A.C.E. your Values**   **How Come?**
3. **Get Motivated**

4. **Know your Audience**
5. **Know your Product**   **How To?**
6. **Develop Skills**

7. **Grow Wiser**
8. **Repeat**   **How Long?**

We provide detailed descriptions and instructions for each
of these eight steps. For now, here is a brief description of how
The Eight Steps can work together.

Steps 1, 2, and 3 are the "How come?" steps. Effective
chapters always begin by understanding their purpose and
developing their own motivation to achieve desired outcomes.
They systematically maximize their chapter's total membership
based on their founding purpose and shared values. Once the
foundation is set (Step 1), members have agreed to Achieving,

Communicating, and Expecting congruent values-based behaviors (Step 2), and they have a unifying dream providing motivational fuel (Step 3), they can then take action to grow the quantity and quality of their chapter brothers.

Next we learn "How to" with Steps 4, 5, and 6. These steps help us develop an understanding of our target audience (Step 4), a deeper knowledge of the value we provide (Step 5), and the interpersonal skills necessary to confidently communicate the organization's values and value to the public (Step 6).

Finally, Steps 7 and 8, the "How long" steps, remind us that long-term sustained growth and success requires us to constantly seek wisdom from external and internal sources (Step 7). Furthermore, long term success is supported by the implementation of repeatable systems and training that instill positive patterns of behavior in all of our members (Step 8).

This eight step system guides you in a sequential learning experience that develops patterns of behavior – habits – for you and your members. As soon as you are familiar with this program, you must do two things:

1. *Practice the principles by putting your plan into action. Go do it!*
2. *Share the program with someone else as it was taught to you. Teach it!*

May you enter the world of limitless possibility fearlessly and with total disregard for the impossible.

THE STAGE IS SET

With the principles we have given you, the stage is now set for you to:

✴ Have an enormous pool of prospects to choose from when building your chapter's membership.

✴ Expand your chapter to a size you've never imagined.

✴ Improve your chapter's image and influence on campus.

✴ Have more money to do more fun things as a chapter.

✴ Simplify your job as a recruiting member of the chapter (especially if you are the Recruitment Chairman).

✴ Increase the quality of your members so that you can be proud of each and every one of them.

✴ Better yourself

This list of benefits is just the start of what The Eight Steps to Limitless Possibility can do for you. But all of the information, training, tips, and tools provided in this book are for naught unless you and your chapter choose to internalize them, and put them into practice. Understand that this is a real opportunity for personal and chapter growth, but the choice is absolutely yours. In other words:

Your opportunity is
N O W H E R E.

What's your interpretation of this statement? Is your opportunity Nowhere or Now Here?

"If you want to change some things in your life, you've got to change some things in your life."

~Dexter Yager~

Step 1: Know the Basics

Major League Baseball is a complex business, but one thing you hear "expert" analysts talking about all the time is the fact that the best teams are built on "pitching and defense." That's quite a statement considering no runs are scored by either pitchers or fielders while they're on defense. Yet, you hear time after time that the experts believe "pitching and defense" to be the fundamentals of a great baseball team.

The suggestion is, then, that when a General Manager builds a baseball team, he should first focus on getting great pitching and great defense – then and only then, should he consider anything else. Home run hitters, base stealers, new stadiums, fancy uniforms, and the flavor of cotton candy sold by the vendors are all secondary details when compared to "pitching and defense." A great baseball team knows the basic components that are necessary to win a championship and they focus on making those basic components – the fundamentals – remarkable.

Even if you're not a baseball fan, you can probably think of parts of your life in which it is important to first focus on the fundamentals – to Know the Basics. So in our fraternity context, before we get into the details of how to build a healthy organization through effective recruitment strategies, we first must understand the very basic fundamentals of fraternities – our organizations' core composition.

The first step in The Eight Steps to Limitless Possibility, Know the Basics, asks you to consider your very make-up as an organization. What makes it tick? What basic needs do you have as a chapter? What has kept you around this long?

The answers to these questions are simpler than you might think. There are two basic needs that make your fraternity tick. There are two basic things that were there at the genesis of the organization and that have kept your fraternity around for decades: **People and Purpose.** Your chapter, just like your organization's founding chapter, needs a bunch of dudes and a reason to get together. If your chapter only had one of these, what would it be?

A group of dudes without a purpose is just a boys club for hanging out.

A purpose without people to fulfill it is just a fluffy idea floating around in space.

Put these two things together though – people and purpose – and what do you get? You get an organization just like your fraternity. What makes any organization unique is its specific purpose and the unique individuals that come together, committed to that purpose.

The process looks something like this: Recruit members, they develop together through the purpose of the organization; those new members recruit more members, and then they develop together through the purpose of the organization. It is an endless cycle, as long as it isn't ignored, and your very lifeblood as a fraternity. This is your very nature, the way that the organization is made.

It only makes sense, then, that this basic, natural set of needs created by the cycle of membership should be concentrated upon and fulfilled before other needs of the organization's own hierarchy. If you focus on recruitment and individual character development more than you focus on what's going to be on next semester's rush T-shirts and who hooked-up with whom at the last social event, you'll start seeing significant positive change. Aren't the fundamentals of people and purpose like the fundamentals of pitching and defense in baseball?

This is pretty simple stuff, we know, but ask yourself this question. What percentage of time at your last chapter meeting was spent talking specifically about a real plan to get more members, and/or how best to develop the character of your current membership so that you will have a higher quality organization? Our experience has shown us that almost all failed fraternity chapters can trace their failure back to a lack of focus on people and purpose.

HOW ARE YOU SPENDING YOUR ENERGY?

The *Pareto Principle*, a brilliantly simple truism from a brilliant economist, states that 80% of the results of any organization usually come from 20% of the effort. Your challenge is, can you flip that upside down?

If you spent 80% of your chapter's energy on the areas of your needs that currently receive about 20% (People and Purpose), wouldn't your chapter's quantity of quality members increase dramatically? And if that happened, wouldn't many of the major headaches chapter leaders experience disappear because you'd have more guys, better guys (who fulfill their commitments, pay their dues, and don't embarrass you), more money, more time, and more sororities that want to hang out with you? Sounds good, right?

You've probably seen chapters on your campus or within your organization that have been closed or reorganized. Almost every time that happens it is because the chapter has strayed from the basics – recruiting the right people and staying true to the purpose of the organization.

Step 1, Know the Basics, is pretty simple, but important nonetheless. We often take for granted the very things that give our fraternity life. Shift your focus. Get more people to achieve the fraternity's purpose. Do what matters first.

DO IT.

Experience the limitless possibilities that await your chapter right away by applying the ideas provided here:

✳ **Evaluate your next chapter meeting. What percentage of time is spent specifically on results producing recruitment activities and fulfillment of the chapter's purpose? Are you as focused as you should be on these basic things?**

✳ **Evaluate your chapter's budget. What percentage of money is spent on things that *actually* grow the chapter in quantity and quality? How much money is fizzled away on less important things?**

✳ **Evaluate your recruitment efforts during the 10 weeks after rush. Are you meeting just as many prospects? Are you putting the same amount of effort into developing relationships with prospective members? Are you extending invitations for membership all semester long? Remember the Pareto Principle.**

✳ **Empower your chapter's Secretary to maintain a journal keeping track of time and resources to make sure that the focus is on the basics – people and purpose.**

"When the values of an organization disappear, the value of an organization disappears."

~unknown~

STEP 2: A.C.E. YOUR VALUES

Step 2 is about the quality of your current and future members. It is also about whether your chapter abides by the "truth in advertising" law.

In this step, your organization re-commits to **Achieving, Communicating,** and **Expecting (A.C.E.)** the values of the fraternity. Doing what you say you'll do as an organization is vital for successful recruitment. After all, who would join a group of hypocrites, liars or con-artists?

In order to not exemplify any of those unflattering terms you must actively exemplify the fraternal values you do espouse. Those values are displayed internally through your rituals, teachings, and code of conduct. Externally, those values are announced loudly through your publications, history and mission statement. People outside of your organization have a predetermined idea of what you are supposed to represent, so you are expected to do what you say you will do. All you have to do as an organization is A.C.E. your values!

1.   Achieving

To achieve one's values, one must first know and embrace them. Once you have pried open the secret closet, blown the dust off the ritual book, and taken a peek inside, take the time to consider what changes in your organization and personal life need to be made in order to know that you are ACHIEVING what your founders hoped for. If you aren't working to achieve your fraternity's values, you may be leading your prospective members into something they aren't expecting.

2.   Communicating

Your words, your outward appearances, and your actions are clearly COMMUNICATING your beliefs. Every minute of every day your members are sending messages to the world about what a fraternity man that wears your letters is all about. This is great, if the message is on target with your stated purpose. What is your chapter communicating?

3.   Expecting

You must also EXPECT the values that you espouse as an organization of your members, and especially of yourself. This means holding each other accountable to the pledges that you make as brothers. Prospective members can tell when a chapter lacks integrity. Do you actually hold your members accountable to the things you say are expected of them?

In recruitment, when you A.C.E. your values, you:
- ✳ Create a better public image
- ✳ Get more brothers involved in recruitment.
- ✳ Prepare your brothers to help others understand your organization (because you understand it).
- ✳ Separate your chapter from other "frats" on campus.
- ✳ Establish a benchmark for identifying quality new members.

SHARE YOUR RITUAL WITH NON-MEMBERS

The thought of sharing your esoteric ritual with non-members probably makes you uneasy, maybe even a little queasy. We know. It's OK, and we'll explain.

At one time, early on, being a secret society was a necessary part of most fraternities' survival. Unfortunately today, uncertainty about which parts of the fraternity are esoteric coupled with a fear of being the one to let out ancient secrets has created a hush so powerful that most fraternity men rarely tell prospective members *anything at all* about what their organization stands for. Worse yet, fraternity men got so good at keeping secrets that many of our own brothers can't even communicate the fraternity's meaning to one another. But, you can change that.

Respect the fraternity's esoteric rituals and traditions (the ones from your founders, not the ones from the 1980's that involve paddles and livestock). This is an important part of your history. However, you also have to build your ability to communicate your core values through words and actions. To help clarify, consider the differences between your fraternity's ceremony, ritual, and values.

Ceremony/Ritual/Values

It is important to ensure we are working with the same terminology as the term values, as we use it, can often be confused with some other common terms. When these eight steps talk about communicating organizational values, it isn't meant to encourage your members to break their pledges of secrecy about esoteric, ritualistic material.

There is a distinct difference between the secret CEREMONIES of the fraternity, the RITUALIZED performance of those ceremonies (periodic reverently performed ceremonies), and the VALUES that form the backbone of the organization.

The words in the ceremonies are only one way to express the values of your fraternity. In fact those ceremonies encourage you to communicate your values through your actions and your character. Even more than that, your ritualistic ceremonies encourage you to literally share the meaning of your organization with others, so that they might find the same value as you have and join.

The ideals, principles, guiding statements, and rules of the organization as identified and set in stone by the founders are called values. A system for creating commitment to these values and communicating a consistent message was established and is called ceremony. Through the ceremony you express what should already be known from your behaviors. The hidden message of the ceremony which tells new candidates the values of your lives that you act out on a daily basis is called ritual. The decisions you make everyday in response to your values separate you from the masses. Hence the fraternal motto, "live your ritual" – suggesting "live your values."

Values	ideas, ideals, rules for living, principles
Ritual	actions, patterns of behavior, expressions
Ceremony	performance, event, play, theater

The commitment to living your values is the foundation of your fraternity's past, present, and future. In a time when the public eye is always watching and the media is quick to provide headlines boasting our fraternal misfortunes, administrators, parents, and students are looking critically at fraternities and asking the question, "What value do you bring to our community?" Your ability, or inability, to perpetuate the timeless values of your ritual will determine your fate, be it prosperity or extinction.

The next time your chapter is sitting around at the end of rush week voting on who should be deemed worthy of getting into the chapter consider the fact that your organization's ritual probably did not demand that you were the perfect man before you were allowed entry into its sacred walls. Most fraternities are actually based on one simple criterion for membership: commitment.

If someday you get a chance to sit down with your ritual book (by the way, the lock on your ritual closet isn't there to keep *you* out), glance in there to see what commitment you have made. You'll find out that all your fraternity asks of its brothers during the pledge process and during their membership is for a commitment to Achieving, Communicating, and Expecting the values of the organization. Essentially, most fraternities are open to any man who is willing to raise his right hand, and say, "Yeah, I'll be your brother for life, act like a decent human being, do nice things for my brothers and the community, pay my dues and not be an idiot."

There are a few challenges, however, that come along with that seemingly simple commitment. You have to know that you're asking that same commitment from all your brothers. You have to communicate that commitment to prospective new members before they join. And, you have to actually live up to your end of the bargain; if one of your brothers breaks that commitment, you must hold them accountable for their actions.

Fraternity is really pretty simple. You promise something to a bunch of guys. They promise the same back to you. Then you hold each other to that promise. If someone breaks the promise, they don't get to play anymore. Simple.

VALUES-BASED SELECTION CRITERIA

Does your chapter have a written set of criteria determining what to look for in a new member? Break away from the "Good Guy" mentality and implement a "Values Based Selection Criteria." Display these criteria during rush events (prospective members should know what you are looking for), use them to decide who is qualified to receive a bid, and make new members aware that they were chosen based on their achievements and character within these standards.

Values	*Standards*
_____	_____
_____	_____
_____	_____
_____	_____
_____	_____
_____	_____

Examples:

Academic Excellence	Has 3.0 or above
Community Service	Has a history of service including 4+ hrs/mo last year
Friendship	Has a meaningful relationship with 3+ brothers who will speak on his behalf

NEW MEMBER COMMITMENTS

What commitments do you ask of your new members? What must each member commit to in order to be your brother?

_____

_____

_____

_____

_____

_____

_____

_____

_____

_____

_____

_____

_____

Examples:

✻ Pay your dues in full and on-time.

✻ Hold a leadership position in at least one other organization on campus.

✻ Attend weekly chapter meetings.

VALUES CASE STUDIES

From the following case studies based on actual events, evaluate the situation and assess the members' activities and decisions based on your core values as well as those of your fraternity. Ask yourself, how will this situation support or compromise our core values? How will I react? Are my chapter's recruitment efforts values-based? Pose these questions to your members and see how the responses differ.

o John is the service chairman of your organization. He has been excited all semester about combining rush with service by holding an event during rush week that raises money to support the local Boys and Girls Club. At your chapter meeting, John stands up to announce that the chapter will be sponsoring a bikini car wash at a gas station on the edge of campus. A different organization did a similar event with sorority girls last semester and raised over $1000 in just one day, plus they got a bunch of new members.

o Pete is a 5th year senior with the most experience in your chapter. He has a great idea for a recruitment/new member activity that he did before he pledged. Pete comes to you with a list of 25 tasks that he will be challenging the chapter's prospective members to complete. The list includes some educational tasks such as looking up questions on the chapter's history in the library and getting personal information from brothers, but also includes some "adventures," as Pete referred to them, such as having girls submit their undergarments and stealing a composite picture from a rival fraternity.

o The chapter needs a fun place to go that will attract new prospects during the week's rush events. Bob's girlfriend works at Hooters and she can get the group a huge discount on food. He reminds all the brothers that last year's Hooters trip was the best turnout of any event they hosted, and this year will be even bigger at only 1/2 the cost.

o To show chapter unity and promote the organization's name, Derrick, an art major, has designed "the coolest rush T-shirts ever." The front displays the fraternity letters and symbols. The back boasts a large picture of a farmer and a bikini girl on a tractor tilling a field with the caption reading, "Pullin' hoes since 1848."

o Mike is a great brother and a pretty good student. Last year Mike took the same History class with the same professor that one of the chapter's newest pledges, Bill, is currently taking. Bill's history midterm is tomorrow morning so he tells the brothers he cannot join them at the Thursday night event with XYZ sorority. Mike says, "wait here" and returns a few minutes later with a copy of the midterm. He gives it to Bill and says, "Now there's no excuse for you not to come have a great time with us."

o   One of the perks of being an upperclassman is having the option to live off campus. This year, two of the chapter's seniors, Kyle and Stan, live in an amazing apartment where they often host parties for brothers and friends. Since the alcohol policies have tightened recently in the chapter house, Kyle comes to the rescue with the announcement that he and Stan will host unrestricted parties for brothers and prospective new members to help get recruitment numbers up this semester.

DO IT.

Experience the limitless possibilities that await your chapter right away by applying the ideas provided here:

* **Does your chapter have a written set of criteria for a prospective new member to receive a bid? Is it more than just being a "good guy?" Get the chapter together and determine your values-based selection criteria.**

* **Are values important? Some brothers argue that the challenge of upholding your collective commitment to an agreed upon values system defines "fraternity." Go find your ritual book and read it to understand what every brother has sworn to live by. Think about how that commitment effects the men you recruit.**

* **Schedule a debriefing session for ALL brothers after any new member ritual ceremony. Use this time to answer questions, discuss the ceremony, identify values, and talk about how/why the chapter exemplifies these founding beliefs.**

* **Use the Case Studies we've provided to spark challenging, values-based discussions with your brothers.**

S.P.A.M.

Have you ever had the pleasant opportunity of cracking open an ice cold can of meat? That's right, we're talking about canned, spiced, efficient, delicious pork and ham cubes.

What comes to mind when we mention "S.P.A.M?" Go ahead, make your own list of words that you think of when you hear "S.P.A.M." Don't just limit yourself to the strange meat product, what about email spam?

Typically, when we ask those questions, we get responses that include the following terms and statements:

Yuck

Disgusting

Canned mush

Annoying

Gelatinous goo

Nasty

Mystery meat

Repetitive

"Not much substance"

Stinky

"Yum, I love that stuff." (There's always one person)

"What is it?"

"A can of nothing"
"What do those letters mean anyway?"
"Leftovers stuffed together"
"You could eat it, but you probably don't want to"
"It's technically food, but... gross"
"I'd rather eat a steak"
"I'd rather eat my own arm"

Most people have a very clear opinion of S.P.A.M. and, most often, it's not a good one. Ironically, the overwhelming majority of Americans have never even tried it. They just "know" it's not for them.

Now, here's a different question. Do you have anyone on your campus that is anti-Greek? Duh... We know you do. Here's a better question. Do you think a few of those words listed above describing salty meat products and billions of annoying emails might be similar to the words that your anti-Greek classmates would use to describe the fraternities on your campus?

Go ahead and read the list again.

It's not a fun analogy, but sadly it works. Many of the fraternities you'll encounter around the country actually *are* rather disgusting, annoying, canned meat, without much substance, living together in a mysterious box with strange letters on the front that nobody understands.

Now consider how those anti-Greek folks might describe your recruitment efforts: repetitive, in your face, strange, annoying tactics to con people into joining something they don't actually want. Sounds a lot like email spam, don't you think?

Now imagine what a dozen S.P.A.M. cans might resemble if we lined them up next to one another... Yep, Fraternity Row on your campus. A bunch of houses lined up that all look the same, with strange letters on the outside and smelly gelatinous goo for members on the inside. Similarly, the majority of Americans have never tried fraternity either, and their preconceived notion is that they "know" what it's all about and they know it's not for them.

S.P.A.M. Village

Anyway, it's just an analogy. The real lesson here is in the acronym with which S.P.A.M. provides us. That acronym describes the reasons for 95% of your fraternity's recruitment problems, and consequently, organizational quality problems. Your recruitment results could dramatically increase with improvement in these four areas: **S**kills, **P**roduct knowledge, **A**udience understanding, and **M**otivation.

With these four road blocks identified, we can get our arms around the recruitment problem and begin addressing the real issues at hand. The reasons you are not at your peak performance is not because the administration is against you, another fraternity uses dirty rush antics, the IFC dropped the ball during rush week, you don't have a house, or any other excuse. These are beyond your control. The only reason you haven't tripled your membership is because your members did not have the Skill, Product knowledge, Audience understanding, or Motivation necessary to succeed. These are things within your control.

STOP S.P.A.M.'ING YOUR CAMPUS

Skills

Having the ability to communicate, socialize, and effectively grow the membership.

Product Knowledge

Having a firm understanding of your fraternity, its value to its members, and its value to the community.

Audience Understanding

Having the awareness of who you want, where he is, and how to find him.

Motivation

Having the drive to do what is necessary to get the results you desire.

Recruitment excellence is on the other side of mastering these four core areas.

New Patterns of Behavior

Have you ever been driving in your car, gotten almost to your destination, and realized you have no idea what occurred during the last 10 minutes of the trip? Have you ever brushed your teeth without giving it any thought at all or tied your shoes without even looking? These are all tasks that took deep concentration and repetitive error when you first learned them. Now you are doing them without thought. This is called a pattern of behavior.

Patterns of behavior are habits formed –voluntarily or involuntarily – from repetition. You can control a learned behavior such as smoking cigarettes, just as you can control behaviors like reading a book before going to bed or shaking hands with strangers. How you make these a repetitive need in your life is up to you, but all can be learned and controlled. Patterns of behavior are present in your life all day, everyday, at your will. When you learn to take charge of these forces you begin taking hold of a powerful force in your daily life.

Psychologists have determined that it takes about 21 days to make or break a habit. In less than a month's time, you could employ new patterns of behavior in your life to transform fraternity recruitment into a seamless part of your day – like tying your shoes. There is no need to spend all of your money and time on big rush events only to get a handful of men. The Eight Steps process empowers you to spread out the effort and spend a lot less money by implementing a system that incorporates the development of positive patterns of behavior in your members.

Patterns of behavior to improve your recruitment results start with reading this book, practicing the ideas in this book everyday for the next 21 days, teaching the ideas in this book to at least one other person, and then re-reading the book again to see what else you may have missed.

We will provide new ideas to use as your patterns of behavior which will overcome your S.P.A.M. issues (lack of Skills, Product knowledge, Audience understanding and Motivation). You have to commit to trying these new behaviors, and practicing them. Let's start with Motivation.

"The world makes way for the man who knows where he is going."

~Ralph Waldo Emerson~

STEP 3: GET MOTIVATED

Every chapter of every fraternity, from their founding class to their alumni group, deals with motivation problems, especially when it comes to motivating members to actively do their part to recruit new people. Remember, motivation is not something you fix, it's something you manage.

The most important thing to understand about motivating others in a group is that most people will work as hard as their dream is important to them. In other words, they are motivated by *their* desires, not yours.

To this end, there is something you can do to motivate your brothers to get fully involved in recruitment and to do their part to grow your organization to its fullest potential. Build a dream.

There is a lot of technical psychology stuff we could throw at you about external and internal motivation, and positive and negative motivation, and how it's really all about some strange attachment to your Oedipus complex, but we won't get into that. Instead, just consider this. Have you ever had a dream? Not a daydream or even a REM induced dream, but one of those dreams that made you believe that you would do anything to achieve it?

Maybe you had the dream of making the basketball team while everyone around you said you were too short or too slow. Maybe you had the dream of attending your future college, but people around you said there was no way you could get admitted there. Maybe you just had a dream of dating that one young lady you'd had your eye on for so long.

You know what we mean. We're talking about a big, motivating, powerful dream that pulls you toward it; one that means so much to you that you would do anything to achieve it.

Do you know the individual dreams of your chapter brothers?

A LESSON ON MOTIVATION

Jake hated rush. Every semester the Rush Chairman would try to get everyone excited about these fake events where everyone acted all nice just to impress a bunch of freshmen. Anyway, Jake wasn't very good at meeting new people and having chit-chat conversations.

Rush week was coming up and Jake was dreading it again. He considered it to be the Rush Chairman's job to recruit new guys and, even if he was supposed to help out, why should he? The chapter always did alright without his help and there just never seemed to be any point in trying.

Jake was sitting around with his buddy, Ted, one afternoon talking about how awesome the upcoming football season was going to be. They attended a Big 10 school and their team was supposed to be incredible this year. As they were talking about how much fun the tailgate parties were going to be and how cool the new student section of the stadium was, Ted had a thought...

"Wouldn't it be cool if we could fill up half the student section with our brothers? Imagine if our chapter had about 400 guys in it, and we all showed up wearing the same T-shirt. We'd be on national television and the whole world could see our domination of this campus.

"You know, Jake, all we'd have to do is have each guy meet like five or six people a day for a week. We could like triple the size of our chapter if we just did it right."

Well, Jake had never considered that it might really be that simple and he had never imagined their chapter dominating a section of the football stadium. How cool would it be to be that powerful on campus? Maybe he would be a little more involved during rush this semester.

And the dream was started...

Does your organization have a dream right now? Does your chapter have something to shoot for? Do your members have a powerful, compelling reason to do the sometimes menial tasks it takes to make your recruitment efforts successful? Have you determined what, as a fraternity chapter, is important enough for all of you to work toward... so important, in fact, that it doesn't matter how much effort is necessary, it will get done?

There is a phenomenon in the fraternity world called "Post-Chartering Blues." This happens when a newly chartered group has worked for a long time to achieve their status as a "chapter." All of the group's efforts have been focused on working to fulfill their dream of becoming an official chapter. Once all the pieces are in place and the group is officially chartered as a chapter, the "Post-Chartering Blues" set in. The group becomes apathetic, bored, and typically smaller. There is a chance that several members will drop out or lose touch with the chapter. Often, the group suddenly stops performing at its highest level.

Almost all new groups experience this phenomenon if they are not counseled through the experience. The cause is very simple. THE GROUP'S ONLY DREAM WAS TO BECOME A CHARTERED CHAPTER. Once that dream was fulfilled, there was nothing else left to work for; there was no MOTIVATION!

The reason for a chapter dream is obvious: You need something to work for. This is what drives your motivation. Once you've developed your dream in detail (the rest of this step can help you do that) and you know that you'll do whatever it takes to achieve that dream as a chapter, you'll find that your brothers will actually show up to events and activities, you'll find you have more volunteers, you'll find that your boys will actually do what they said they would do, and they are more than happy to do all these things because the dream is as important to them as it is to you.

BUILD YOUR DREAM

Choosing to build your dream takes two key principles:

1. *There can be no limits on your dream. Imagine a world of limitless possibilities.*

2. *Choose a positive attitude. Choose an attitude of "Yes we can!"*

Now, it is time to build your dream. Take some time for yourself right now to write down your own dream. There are some questions on the following pages to help you through this exercise. Once you've written down your personal dream, you've completed the first part of the process. Next, do this exercise with your entire chapter, with your new member education classes, and even with your potential members to see what it is that gets them motivated.

There will be no more excuses as to why your chapter brothers are not motivated to do their part in recruitment. You will have the dream that drives your efforts from here forward.

To begin the exercise, start to imagine those late night conversations that you've had with other members of your chapter. Remember those conversations? They start with: *"Wouldn't it be great if our chapter...."* You fill in the blank.

That's the beginning of a dream.
Now take it further.

Pull out a few blank sheets of paper and answer the following questions. Spend some time pushing yourself to brainstorm (with no limitations... limitless possibilities) all the details of your dream. The bigger the better.

What would your chapter be able to HAVE if it had as many high quality men as it wanted?
(Think about tangible things that you can touch.)

What would your chapter be able to DO because of all those high quality men?
(Think about activities, trips, events, and other stuff you can do.)

What would your chapter BECOME as a result of having as many high quality men as it wanted?
(Think about how you will see yourself as a result of your fulfilled dream. How will others see you? What does your chapter become once your dream is achieved?)

A long time ago a young man had a dream to start your fraternity. Look what has happened since then!

What do you dream about? Are you brave enough to dream bigger and better than your contemporaries? Are you smart enough to share your dream with your brothers and write it down like your founders did?

DREAM BUILDERS

Some people are great at dreaming big. Others need a little help. Consider doing the following with your chapter brothers to help build your dream as big as it can be.

✳ Take a road trip to the biggest chapter in your fraternity at another college or university.

✳ Attend a national or regional fraternity event.

✳ Find a fraternity's chapter composite picture that has 100 men or more in it and post a copy of it in your house or meeting area.

✳ Calculate what your chapter's budget could be if it had three times the members it has today.

✳ Calculate the service hours and philanthropic dollars that a chapter twice your current size could accumulate.

✳ Take a tour of a fraternity house that holds 80 or more men.

✳ Call your fraternity's national headquarters and ask them to tell you about the biggest and best chapters in the country.

PLEASURE VS. PAIN PRINCIPLE

Eighteenth century British philosopher Jeremy Bentham first introduced the Pleasure/Pain Principle when he suggested that all men act in accordance with the pursuit of pleasure or the avoidance of pain.

Within the context of fraternity, we can motivate ourselves and others by not only building big pleasurable dreams, but also by attaching exciting rewards and painful consequences to the actualization of those dreams.

As a recruitment example, a brother might choose you as his "accountability buddy" and agree to introduce himself to five new men on campus for five consecutive days. He turns over his video games to you and may only reclaim them after the completion of his goal. The keys to making this form of motivation work are 1) a true accountability buddy, 2) a worthwhile attainable goal, 3) an exciting reward and painful consequence, and 4) check points of progress along the way.

THE CURE FOR APATHY IS RECRUITMENT

Once upon a time, a farmer gave each of his three sons a baby mule and a plot of land. Years later, the brothers sat together discussing the lazy, stubborn disposition of their animals.

The first brother complained, "I got so fed up I bought a whip and beat my mule until he obeyed me."

The second brother replied, "I tried the whip but learned that dangling a carrot in front of him is slightly more effective."

The youngest brother calmly interrupted, "I use neither the whip nor the carrot and enjoy pleasant rides to and from the marketplace."

"How is this possible?" cried the elder brothers.

"I traded my mule for a horse."

Consider the time you invest in trying to find carrots and sticks to use on the *asses* in your chapter. With a fraction of that time, how many "horses" could you personally recruit that would eagerly lead the chapter the way you do?

Always leave the door open to your apathetic members; invite them to get more involved and praise them when they do so. However, be mindful that the best solution to your apathy problems is usually excited, passionate, quality new members.

DO IT.

Experience the limitless possibilities that await your chapter right away by applying the ideas provided here:

* **Spend an upcoming chapter meeting or retreat building your chapter's collective dream. Start by letting individual members build their fraternal dream. Then, do it collectively to see what everyone wants to achieve together.**

* **Realize that each brother is motivated by something entirely unique. If you want to motivate your brothers, or hold them accountable, ask them what the best way to do that is. Develop a spreadsheet of each brother's Pains and Pleasures based on their own recommendations.**

* **Use the Have, Do, Become exercise for everything you truly want to achieve (maybe a degree or a job) and post your written dream on your bathroom mirror for daily review. Harvard studies have shown this to be extremely powerful.**

* **Build recruitment teams of 2-5 brothers to support each other and serve as accountability buddies.**

"What we see depends mainly on what we look for."

~John Lubbock~

What do you see?

STEP 4: KNOW YOUR AUDIENCE

Before we start Step 4, take a moment to consider this scenario and the question at the end of it.

Your Campus President's Speech

The president of your school is about to announce his top initiative – a plan to dramatically enhance student life. He has called together a group of 100 non-Greek, male students that perfectly match the school's demographic mix. There is an overwhelming feeling of anticipation as the importance of this message has been rumored for days. Several long minutes pass. The lecture room's large doors open abruptly as the President enters and walks quickly toward the podium with a stern expression of importance on his face. After looking over the audience one time, he begins ...

Thank you for joining me today. What I am about to present to you, I hope you will consider a great honor and therefore give much thought. From a campus of many, you are a few – hand selected by those who think you to be of high character, exemplary leadership, and extraordinary potential.

Our community, our nation, and even the world are in a time of great change and challenge. This school has a rich history of excellence, producing some of America's premier leaders. Beginning immediately, we will aggressively move forward toward creating a culture that consistently produces world class achievement.

It is the philosophy of this institution to build our model for success from the ground up. Therefore, the future of this movement will begin with you. An organization of our top undergraduates will be assembled by students, for students – an organization deeply rooted in core values and built in partnership with those peers whom you deem worthy to share such an honor.

The challenges will be many, but the rewards will be eternal. Know that this task brings with it great honor that will yield for you life-long relationships and personal growth. Your best efforts will be supported by the university, faculty, staff, and community. And, as a result, you will have made an impact far beyond your temporary stay as an undergraduate.

If you wish to explore this opportunity in further detail, I ask that you rejoin me in this same room in half an hour. Thank you.

Based on the realities of your campus, how many of the 100 men will return?

Interested Men: _____

(Remember this number; you're going to use it again in just a few minutes)

Now, one more bit of knowledge before we go too much further. A while back some researchers determined that on average, most college campuses have three types of men that show up on the first day of their freshman year.

✳ **"Always Joiners."** Statistically, 15% of men report being "likely to join a fraternity" when surveyed early in their freshmen year.

✳ **"Never Joiners."** An estimated 15% of the male population is adamantly opposed to joining Greek life. These fraternity-haters would not accept a bid if it came with a Porsche and tickets to the Super Bowl.

✻ **"Maybe Joiners."** Approximately 70% of the male
population does not know or does not care a whole lot about
fraternities. They could be convinced to join if it was
proposed the right way.

THREE TYPES OF PROSPECTIVE MEMBERS

Always Joiners = 15%
Never Joiners = 15%
Maybe Joiners = 70%

Which group are you targeting?

So, we've got three types of people. Remember those
percentages, because we'll need to use them in a minute. It's
probably worth mentioning that you might be like us. When we
showed up at college, we said, "There's no way I'm ever joining
one of those dumb frats." Now we're writing a book about
fraternities. While we thought we were "Never Joiners" we were
actually "Maybe Joiners," but we just didn't know it.

Alright, time for some math.

Who loves math? You? Great! You'll really enjoy this next bit of fun we've provided for you. Take out your pencil and calculator and try the equations found on the next two pages out for size.

Write down the population of your undergraduate student body on Line A

_____   Line A

Subtract the number of female students from your student body population, and put the number of males on Line B.

- # of women on campus

_____   Line B

Great! Now, subtract the number of men already in fraternities on your campus from Line B, and put the answer on Line C.

- # of Current Fraternity Men

_____   Line C

Great! Now, from Line C, subtract 15% (**"Never Joiners"**), and write that new number on Line D.

_____ - 15%

_____ Line D

Line D is your prospective pool of membership. Now, use this number for the next part of the math fun.

Remember that number you came up with after "The President's Speech?" Write that number down on line E.

_____% Line E

Use your calculator to figure out what Line E times Line D equals, and put the solution on Line F. (For instance, if Line D says 200 and, Line E says 25%, then Line F equals 50)

_____ **Line F**

This exercise demonstrates that if you were to present your fraternity to prospective members in the same meaningful way that the president presented his new campus organization to those 100 male students, you would have dramatically improved interest. On your campus, the number of men on line F would be interested in a conversation about the benefits of fraternity life.

We've done this hundreds of times with all types of campuses. If your math isn't showing you that you've got a lot more potential than you are currently achieving, you probably did your math wrong. Most chapters find out that they could be getting dozens, if not hundreds (sometimes even thousands), of new members each year. Or at least they could have that many people to choose from.

Regardless of your school's size, location, Greek population, and so on, this equation shows that there is a lot of potential out there for your organization. You just have to go find it. The results are hidden within the "maybe joiners." They won't come to you. You have to go to them.

MATH EXAMPLE

Take this example of a campus with:

* ✳ 5,000 Total Students
* ✳ 50% Female Population
* ✳ 300 Fraternity Men
* ✳ 15% Never Joiners
* ✳ 40% would come back after President's Speech

$$5,000 - 50\% = 2,500$$
$$2,500 - 300 = 2,200$$
$$2,200 - 15\% = 1,870$$
$$1,870 \times 40\% = 748$$

Each chapter on this campus has the potential to recruit 748 people this semester. What if they could get just 10% of their potential to join in one semester (74 guys!)?

Remember, even if you don't want that many members in your chapter, *Quantity drives Quality*. The more prospects you have the more chance you have to get the highest quality members into your chapter.

So, how do you find those people? That's a great question.

SIX WAYS TO FIND PROSPECTIVE MEMBERS

Here's a quick, important reminder: You can't recruit those you haven't met.

There is a lot to recruiting great guys, and we'll get to all of that, but it is absolutely true that you just plain can't recruit who you don't know. Maybe you could, but that wouldn't get the quality results you are looking for. So, here are six ways that you can get NAMES. That's all we're talking about here. We need to get the names of as many people as possible on a list (we'll call that a "Names List"), from there we can work on building the relationship, and maybe, if all the stars align, we can ask some of them to join. First we need to get a ton of names on a list.

We like to say that quantity drives quality. The more names you can accumulate, the better chance you'll have of getting high quality members.

There are six general ways to maximize your list of prospective members' names. Ask yourself if your chapter is using all of these methods as effectively as possible. Or, as one member put it, "are you running on all six cylinders?"

+--+
| **IS YOUR CHAPTER RUNNING ON** |
| **ALL 6 CYLINDERS?** |
| |
| 1. Referrals |
| 2. Summer Recruitment |
| 3. Member Positioning |
| 4. Membership Drives |
| 5. Marketing For Names |
| 6. Rush |
+--+

1. Referrals

Begin by using the "Mind Joggers" we've provided near the end of this chapter to get referrals from yourself and current members. The average member can generate 50+ names with minimal effort. Ask for referrals of top undergraduates from sorority leaders, faculty members, administrators, alumni brothers, and other organization leaders. Also, consider using new technology with websites that link new friends together.

2. Summer Recruitment

Each campus is a bit different, but all have some potential for summer recruitment. Consider leveraging incoming freshman lists from the Admissions Department. Tap into freshmen prospects through guidance counselors at targeted high schools. Also think about using regional events for incoming students, such as orientations or information sessions, as ways to be the first to meet future students. If you have a short list of incoming/returning student prospects, home visits are another great way to set your fraternity apart from others and show that you are really interested in those gentlemen. Remember, the goal is simple, meet them and start building a friendship.

3. Member Positioning

Every member of the chapter should be involved in multiple campus organizations and leadership roles. Encourage members to get involved in residence life, admissions work, orientation programs, campus tours, recreation center/intramurals, and so forth. Use rosters and contact sheets from these activities to build your Names List.

4. Membership Drives

Rush week is not the only time to have a membership drive, and those drives can take various forms. Consider making a post-rush push, mid-semester drive, or end of the semester clean up. Many chapters find success with techniques such as dorm storming, "5 for 5", information tables, activities fairs, and move in/out days.

"5 for 5" is simple, and it's one of the most effective ways we've found to dramatically increase your Names List. If you do

"5 for 5," there is a good chance you'll get more men through this effort than you've ever gotten from one of your big rush events.

"5 for 5" is a challenge. Are you willing to meet, just meet, 5 new men a day for the next 5 days?

If you are willing to take that challenge, and make that commitment, you alone can grow your fraternity's prospective membership pool by 25 people. If 4 of your brothers take that challenge with you, then your chapter will grow its prospect list by 125 people within only 5 days. How many of your big rush events have ever resulted in personal conversations with 100+ men? **Start "5 for 5" today and you'll see results immediately.**

5. Marketing for Names

The important thing to remember about marketing is that an effort that does not produce names can be good for public relations, but without names, you've got no *real* results. Market your chapter in ways that will put names on the list. Consider promoting academic scholarships, hosting a banquet, sports league involvement, soliciting for involvement in a service/philanthropy opportunity, parent solicitations, and other similar opportunities.

6. Rush

Traditional campus-organized "rush" is the most commonly used method for gathering names. Participate in the programming and maximize its potential, but realize that you are reaching only a very small percentage of your prospect pool during this traditional, static, and formal rush process. Remember to gather names throughout the process. This is a great way to pump up your Names List with men who have already expressed interest in Greek life. Don't forget to revisit last year's rush list for quality men who have not yet joined a fraternity.

Whatever methods you end up using to build your Names List, Step 4 is really about seeing your chapter's potential and shifting your efforts to build as many personal relationships as possible with the men on your campus. Success, beyond your expectations, is available right now. And that's without even mentioning the non-traditional members that could join your organization if asked: graduate students, professors, university staff, local gentlemen, your members' fathers, the Chief of Police, the campus religious leaders, and many others.

You have limitless potential.

M<small>IND</small> J<small>OGGERS</small>

Creating your own Names List is the critical first step in developing a successful recruitment system. The larger the Names List gets, the more successful you'll become. You'll have a greater opportunity to recruit more QUALITY individuals when you increase the size of your prospective membership pool. Put EVERYONE on the Names List!

Here's how it's done:

Write down everyone you know on the Names List. Use this list of mind joggers to ensure you have exhausted your network of connections. DO NOT PREJUDGE ANYONE. Put everyone on the list. Now is not the time to decide if someone is qualified for membership.

Pull out a big piece of paper (or create a simple computer spreadsheet) and get ready to write down names. You may want to use the space at the end of this book to start your Names List.

Turn the page, and GO!

Write down all the...

Men you know who...

* Are scholars

* Are leaders on campus

* Are service minded

* Are loyal

* Are gentlemen

* Want to succeed in life

* Value family and friends

* Make you laugh

Men you know who...

* Were/are in your freshman hall (all of them)

* Currently live on your floor or in your building

* Are on your sports team (all of them)

* Are on your intramural teams

* Are in the same clubs/organizations you are (get a roster)

* Exemplify pride in your school

* Are residence life advisors on campus

* Work with you at your job(s)

* Spend all their time in the computer lab

* Spend all their time in the library

* Are spiritually driven

* Sit with you at lunch/dinner
* Sit within 2 tables of you at lunch/dinner
* Sit within 10 seats of you in class (do this for every class)
* Sat within 10 seats of you in class last semester (do this for every class)
* Are already an officer for another group on campus
* Workout in the gym/weight room
* Always sit in the front of the class
* Have traveled abroad
* Did not get accepted into/dropped out of another fraternity

Now check the following resources for additional names:

* Your cell phone speed dial listing
* Your written address book/Palm Pilot
* Student directory
* List of all freshman males (from admissions office/student affairs)
* Rosters for clubs and organizations
* IFC sign up sheets (prior years as well)
* Last year's yearbook
* Housing lists
* Rosters for athletics/sports teams

* Invitation lists from socials, formals, and etc.
* Email lists/list serves
* Instant message buddy lists

Men you may not have considered...

* Seniors you know
* Commuters
* Adult students
* Professors
* Your freshman year RA
* Graduate students
* ROTC cadets
* International students
* That guy who never leaves his room
* University professionals/staff
* Your closest friend's friends

GREAT JOB!

RECRUITS RECRUITING

Who knows more freshmen than other freshmen? Who is more excited about your fraternity than your newest members or eager prospects?

Empower your prospects and new members with the message that they are the future of your fraternity. Let them know that now is the time for them to start being a leader. Ask them to look everywhere, including their classes, dorm, and teams, to find the men they want to join them on their fraternal adventure. Ask them to help build their own new member class.

Some chapters even go a step further and require their newest members to recruit at least one other new member before being initiated.

As an example, a fraternity chapter of 35 brothers at a mid-size Ohio school used the ideas in this book to recruit 22 men in the early part of one year's fall semester. Two months later, they were ready to initiate 35 new men into the organization (doubling the size of their chapter).

How did they do it? When asked how they went from 22 pledges to 35 initiates, they replied, "We were taught that we can recruit year-round. So we told our pledge class to recruit another class of men who they want to be their brothers. It turns out they're better recruiters than we are."

DO IT.

Experience the limitless possibilities that await your chapter right away by applying the ideas provided here:

* **Use the equation for calculating your school's pool of prospects with your chapter. Once your members see the numbers, teach them about the six cylinders and how to get those "maybe joiners."**

* **Make a 5 day growth plan with 4 of your best friends in the fraternity. Commit to "5 for 5." Determine some sorority women and other classmates, professors, staff, and others from whom you could ask for referrals. Run through the Mind Joggers and figure out all the other small ways you could grow your chapter in just 5 days.**

* **Start a real Names List. Develop a spreadsheet using your favorite database software (Microsoft Excel® is fine), and include a column for names, phone numbers, email addresses, notes, and etc. You can find an example online at: http://www.PhiredUp.com/**

* **Empower your new members and even your aspiring prospects to recruit right away.**

"Knowledge is a process of piling up facts; wisdom lies in their simplification."

~Martin Fischer~

Step 5: Know Your Product

So far we've tackled Steps 1 and 2, which set the foundation for a successful chapter. Then, we hit Steps 3 and 4, which explained the M (Motivation) and A (Audience understanding) in our S.P.A.M. acronym. Now, we've got four more steps left in which to cover Product knowledge, Skills, and some other ideas that'll help you keep up your success for years and years to come.

Moving on to Step 5, the Know Your Product step, brings up a story we heard recently. It's about a door-to-door vacuum salesman (yeah, we didn't think people actually did that anymore either). Anyway, the salesman had just started the job and so far nobody had answered their doors when he had knocked. Finally, it looked like he was going to get lucky with the next house on his route. He could hear the sound of a woman inside shouting, and he thought, just maybe, that he could swoop in and save the day.

The vacuum salesman knocked on the door. The woman clumsily opened it and greeted him with a kind smile that barely hid her frustrated, furled brow. She was curvy and attractive, but that's a different part of the story that we won't get into right now.

"Hi there," she said. "Sorry about the mess and the shouting. My vacuum cleaner just broke, I can't fix it, and I'm all worked up. How can I help you?"

Well, obviously, the salesman had hit the jackpot. So, he sprung into action. "Ma'am, I'm here to help. I'm a vacuum salesman, and I'd like to sell you this vacuum."

"How nice," she said, looking interested in the vacuum and the salesman. "Obviously, I'm a lady in need of your services, but I'll need to know a little about this vacuum first."

This was the vacuum salesman's first time, remember, and he hadn't prepared quite as much as maybe he should have. "Ma'am, well... uhh... as you can see here, the vacuum I have to sell you is... uh... well, it's green. And... uhh... well, it sucks."

That's the end of the story. We didn't say it was a good one. But, we might be able to learn a valuable lesson from our young vacuum salesman friend. If you don't know your product, you're probably not going to be able to sell it. In our fraternity context, if you don't know the value and benefits of your fraternity and you don't know what sets your fraternity apart from all the other organizations on campus, then you'll probably have a very hard time convincing people to join it – even those who need it most.

Imagine for a moment that you are in an elevator within a very tall building on your campus. You're all alone in that elevator until another guy steps in right at the last minute on your way down to the first floor. The guy who just jumped on the elevator with you happens to be the one guy on campus that you think exemplifies what a perfect brother in your fraternity would be like – except none of your guys really know him well and you've never really hung out with him. You've always assumed he wasn't interested in joining a fraternity.

This guy is President of three organizations on campus (including the student government), he's extremely popular, great at sports, has tons of smart and attractive people that follow him around, and he's just an all-around *good guy*.

So there you are on the elevator, with about 30 seconds until you reach the bottom floor, when he says, *"Hey, you're in that fraternity right? Tell me, what's that all about?"*

Quick, what's your response?

If you said something like, *"Well... uhh... we're the green house on the corner and... uhh... we've got the tightest brotherhood on campus,"* you might as well have been the vacuum salesman exclaiming how his product sucks.

There is one major question that Step 5 asks:

1. *Can you help a prospective member see how membership in the fraternity will benefit him? (This means knowing how to communicate the VALUE of your organization.)*

We talk a lot about values in the plural sense in the fraternity world, but unfortunately we don't often talk about just pure value. What value do you offer your members? What value does your organization offer you? Why is it worth the investment of time, energy, passion and money to join your organization? What is the ROI (return on investment)?

If you start to answer those questions with statements like, *"We have an awesome intramural football team,"* or *"We have the nicest house on campus,"* or *"We do all sorts of service and philanthropy work,"* or even, *"We have the tightest brotherhood on campus"* then we have bad news for you. That's not going to be worth the investment for most prospective members.

First of all, all of those statements, and those that sound similar to them, are exactly what every other fraternity on your campus is saying. Secondly, those statements are explaining features and people don't invest their money, time, energy, or passion into features. People invest in the benefits that the features of your organization provide to them.

The difference between a feature and a benefit is sometimes a little fuzzy, but it might help to refer back to our vacuum salesman friend. If he had mentioned that his vacuum was green, it sucks, it has hoses in the back, and a long cord to plug into the wall, he would have been explaining the features of his machine. In order to help him explain the benefits instead of the features, we might encourage him to mention that it reduces the nice lady's cleaning time by 50%, which gives her more time to spend with her hobbies. Also, the long cord and hoses on the machine are ergonomically designed to reduce back strain, which makes cleaning less painful.

The nice lady probably wouldn't buy green sucky hoses and cords, but she might buy more time with her hobbies and a less painful back.

Next time you have a big rush event on campus where you publicly and proudly display your IM basketball trophies, photo albums, and banners, ask yourself if you're displaying features or benefits. If you tell a passerby about your sweet basketball team or that killer party last semester, you're explaining features. They won't invest their time into those features, because they're yours, not theirs. Instead, ask them what they want to get out of their college experience and help them see how they can benefit from what your fraternity has to offer.

Identity Crisis?

One other important task to accomplish in Step 5 is to learn how to handle excuses. You've got to know your product well enough to be able to get around all those excuses which inevitably pop up when asking your prospective members to join.

You know what the excuses will be for not joining your fraternity. You've heard them before because they're the same every semester. What you need to do is be prepared with a surefire way to get past these excuses.

Feel * Felt * Found. These three little words will guide your honest, authentic, quality responses and provide a framework for handling these excuses in the future.

Take one of the most common excuses, for example. *"I don't want to get hazed."* Upon hearing this, you might respond:

*"I know how you **feel**. I **felt** the same way before I joined. I was really scared by all the hazing I had seen in movies and on television. What I **found**, however, was that these guys are actually the opposite of all that. We're actually against hazing. We work really hard to get it out of our fraternity community and our new member education program is really just based on learning how to be a good leader."*

It is important to tell the truth in your response and to speak from your experience. Now think, if you can prepare every member of your chapter with those three words, and they all practiced and prepared to combat these excuses, wouldn't you be able to hang on to a lot more prospects?

No doubt you'll encounter excuses like these and the following examples. But be prepared to get to the heart of the prospect's concerns by using quality responses. Remember Feel * Felt * Found. You'll be amazed at the results.

TOP 10 EXCUSES FOR NOT JOINING YOUR CHAPTER

1. I don't want to get hazed.
2. I can't afford it.
3. My parents don't want me to join.
4. I have to focus on my studies.
5. Upperclassmen don't join fraternities.
6. I don't want to be a stereotype.
7. I don't want to live in a fraternity house.
8. I don't want to be one of those "drunken frat guys."
9. I don't have the time.
10. I have other friends already.

Step 5 is simple. Understand the value that your fraternity has to offer, and be prepared to be able to share that with anyone who wants to hear about it.

QUALITY RESPONSE EXAMPLES

I don't want to get hazed.
  a. Hazing is unacceptable and strictly forbidden in our fraternity.
  b. Let me introduce you to our newest initiates. Feel free to ask them about any details of their pledge period.
  c. Here is our pledge education program outlining everything we do.

I can't afford it.
  a. Do you know how much it costs?
  b. May I show you exactly how much it costs and how that compares to other college expenses?
  c. If we could arrange a payment plan, would that make a difference?

My parents don't want me to join.
  a. What is it they do not approve of?
  b. Why do you think they feel that way?
  c. Have they met any of the members in this fraternity?
  d. Would you be willing to help me arrange an opportunity for them to meet some of the members/members' parents/chapter advisor?

I've got to focus on my studies.
  a. What are your concerns?
  b. Did you know the chapter has minimum standards for maintaining membership in the organization, an academic excellence program, and a program to reward scholastic achievement?
  c. May I introduce you to our scholarship chairman?

You can create responses for the rest of the concerns.

DO IT.

Experience the limitless possibilities that await your chapter right away by applying the ideas provided here:

* **Build your chapter's "Elevator Pitch." In 30 seconds, can you verbalize the value and benefits of being a member of your fraternity?**

* **Read through your chapter's website, brochures, T-shirts, and any other written materials to make sure that they refer to the *benefits* of membership, not just the features.**

* **Prepare quality responses to the Top 10 Excuses for not joining (try putting them on flashcards). Make sure all of your members do the same and, then, practice them together regularly.**

* **Remember back when you told your parents and other special family members about joining the fraternity. How did you explain it to them? Often that's the best way to explain it to others.**

"A true friend is the most precious of all possessions and the one we take the least thought about acquiring."

~La Rochefoucauld~

STEP 6: DEVELOP SKILLS

Warning. This section of the book is one of the longest, but it is also one of the most important. You're going to work on your people skills, which we all know can be a little scary. Don't worry, you'll be fine. We won't be too hard on you. Be prepared to learn, take your time, and don't forget to practice.

To begin with, you already know that the best men on your campus are probably not going to approach you about joining the fraternity. So, you must be wondering, "How exactly do I meet them?" This step, if practiced, can magically transform your members into recruitment machines by teaching them some basic people skills along with some advanced techniques to take your recruiting to the next level.

Remember, the more people you meet, the better your chapter will be.

THE MAGIC OF MEETING PEOPLE

Let's start with a magic trick… You can make anyone in the world concentrate entirely on you, submit their full name, and reveal critical, personal information at your will. All you have to do is look at them first, walk within five feet of where they are, and stick out your right hand. Say the magic words, *"Hi, I'm Bob Smith."* (Substitute your own name for maximum effect) And… PRESTO! A personal conversation begins and the information begins pouring out. By an unknown force, the other guy grasps your hand, begins shaking it, and offers more information about himself than you could have bargained for.

Ridiculous? This is the single most effective skill of top performing statesmen, salesmen, philanthropists, journalists, and even professional recruiters. It may not be much of a "magic trick," but it is the best way to meet a new friend. After all, that's all we are interested in during this early stage. We aren't talking about the fraternity or trying to sell our organization to anyone. All we want to know is if this person is someone we'd like to learn more about. That means having a basic conversation with him.

Once you've introduced yourselves to one another, you're no longer strangers, so loosen up! You may, however, need a couple of good kick off lines to get the conversation rolling. To help out, here are a few options:

- Comment on something he's wearing, carrying, or doing:

"I noticed the cleats in your bag, are you on the soccer team?"

- Comment on a current or upcoming event that you may have in common:

"Did you see the concert on campus this past weekend?"

- Ask for assistance with something you're doing or somewhere you're going:

"I'm looking for a few volunteers to help a group I'm with raise money for a local humane society. Do you know anyone who might be interested in something like that?"

Now, before we go much further, here's a quick question: Have you ever met a beautiful woman for the second or third time, been interested in getting to know more about her, but you couldn't remember her name? It happens all the time. We'll meet someone – especially if it's someone we're interested in – and we'll introduce ourselves, and immediately our mind wanders off to what we're going to say next so that we can seem cool. The problem is that we never hear the other person's name, and by the time we realize this snafu, it is too late to do anything about it and maintain that all important sense of pride.

So, when you're out there making friends, don't forget that his name is the most important word in his vocabulary. Learning that one single word makes all the difference in the world to him, and he will remember you for it. Invest your energy and concentration into memorizing his name.

Here's the best way to do that. After he says his name, repeat it in your next sentence, think of it again in your head, associate it with something about him (to help it "stick"), and then use it again when you say "good-bye."

CONVERSING FOR RESULTS

Congratulations! You're half way there.

So far, you've approached somebody that you would normally walk right past, and you've used the secret magic trick to break the ice and learn a little about them. You know the most important word in their language. Your lead-in question got you started. But there always seems to be that awkward moment of silence when nobody knows exactly what to say, right? Stay confident, you can forget about that F*'n problem from now on.

The best way to remain confident is to control the conversation. The best way to control the conversation is to monopolize the listening. The best way to monopolize the listening is to ask open-ended questions about him. The best way to communicate that you really care about someone is to intently listen to them speak – and the best part is that you don't have to do much talking at all.

Check out the Five F*'n ways to Master Conversation on the next page.

The object of these F*'n ways to master conversation is to provide you with open-ended question topics that build rapport and establish common interests or experiences. Stay in control, offer a little about yourself, and always go back to talking about him.

FIVE F*'N WAYS
TO MASTER CONVERSATION

Just ask about ...

Family/Friends
How do you know John? How close are you with your family? Who else is on the team? How did you guys meet? How does your family feel about ...?

Favorites
I love Tony's Pizza, what do you normally order?
Which classes are your favorites?
Which sports teams do you follow?

Firsts
What do you think of Freshman Seminar so far?
How is your first week of classes going? What was your first impression of this place?

Fun
I love poker too, how often do you play cards? What other card games do you know? Where do you guys usually hang out on the weekends? What else are you involved in outside of class?

From
Where are you from? How did you end up here?
Where do you live now? How often do you get back to Florida? What was it like growing up in...?

Great job! You've survived a few minutes of good conversation with a complete stranger. It's time to bring the discussion to a temporary close. Remember, you are leading the conversation. While your opening line worked great to get the conversation going, we need a similar line to transition out of the conversation without cutting off the new relationship forever. Remember, the idea is to get back together in the near future. Try something like this:

- *I'd love to keep talking with you, but I need to get going. Maybe we can grab lunch together sometime.*
- *Thanks for the information, maybe we can talk more later.*
- *I have some other commitments I need to get to, let's talk again soon.*

Warning! Critical point! This is not the time to exit. Leaving the conversation without any contact information or a time to meet up again leaves you with nothing to show for your efforts. It's imperative that you walk away with an appointment and/or a way to reach your new friend. To help do this tactfully, here's another magic trick:

You say, *"Before I get going, here's my contact information.* [Write it down on a scrap piece of paper with him in front of you.] *Give me a call if you'd like to get together* [while offering your information to him]. *Hey, do you have a number where I can reach you?"*

Abra Cadabra! You have contact information for another prospect – and your Names List just grew. You're becoming quite a recruitment Houdini. Another great option is to invite him to an upcoming activity. For example:

You say, *"What time are you eating dinner tonight?* [He responds, "6 o'clock."] *I'm going to be at the food court with some friends around 6 o'clock. You have to eat, don't you?* [It's OK to ask questions you already know the answers to.] *Great, since I'm going to be on campus around that time anyway, I'll drop by your dorm around 5:45 to pick you up. What room number are you in?* [The question wasn't, "Do you want me to pick you up?" The question was, "What room number are you in?"] *Here's my phone number in case your plans change. What's the best way I can reach you when we're on our way?"* [You just got his contact info. Great job.]

Magic trick #3: Get your top hat and rabbit ready for this one. You're about to double or even triple your productivity with two sentences. Here they come...

You say, *"Do you have a roommate?"* [You know he does if he lives in a dorm]. *"Why don't you go ahead and invite him along with you?"* [He's thinking, "Great, I don't have to meet a group of strangers by myself, what a nice guy." You're thinking "Bingo, I just hit the two-for-one jackpot."]

At the conclusion of your meal, event, study group, gathering, or whatever you choose to use as the meet-and-greet session for introducing your new friend(s) to your current friends (brothers), you'll need to do another transition. Don't over think it. You already have his contact info (if you don't, get it now), all you need to do is invite him to join you and more of your cool friends for the next gathering.

Always set up a follow up meeting, pick him up if possible, and make a follow up phone call after the meeting. Getting that commitment to another meeting is critical. It's a little more work than you may be used to, but then again the results are going to be a lot bigger than you're used to as well.

BEYOND THE FIRST MEETING

Now, here is where we could include a section discussing how to be a good friend. That would be a long section, though, and you probably have managed to make one or two friends on your own over the course of your life, so we'll spare you. But remember, that's all you have to do at this point. Make a friend. Be a friend. Hang out. Do normal stuff with all these new people you've met. Involve your fraternity brothers in the fun stuff you and your new friends do. Involve your new friends in the fun stuff your fraternity brothers do. Don't overcomplicate things. You don't need a huge event, a paintball outing, or a raging party to make friends. Just do normal friend stuff.

Reminder:		
Effective Recruitment	$\neq$	*Big Event*

If you need help thinking of normal friend stuff, try some of the ideas we've included on the next page. Doing these every day activities can take the place of your huge rush events or, at least, compliment your huge rush events throughout the rest of the year. Do activities, not events. You'll save money, you'll get to know your prospective members more closely, and you'll seem more like a normal person instead of a scary frat guy who only knows how to talk to people when he's at a kegger.

NORMAL FRIENDLY ACTIVITIES

* Poker Night
* Breakfast/Coffee/Lunch/Dinner (Everybody has to eat!)
* Flag Football
* Watching Sports
* Bar/Party (We're not talking about recruiting at a bar or party, we're talking about being a friend, and doing normal stuff.)
* Service/Philanthropy Events
* Study (There's a novel idea)
* Video Games
* Social Events
* Bowling
* Movies
* Hiking
* Laundry
* Other Campus Activities
* Just "Hanging Out"

You get the idea. Do normal activities together. That's how real friendships are formed. The skills you need to recruit people into your organization are oddly similar to the skills you need to recruit a date for next weekend. You do things like introduce yourself, remember their name, talk about normal stuff, ask for their number, and set up a time to meet again soon. You wouldn't immediately ask your prospective date on your first meeting to join you at a barbecue where there'll be about 20 other prospective mates that you'll be judging to deem their worthiness of your manhood. No, you would do normal things and get to know the person. It's really pretty simple.

At some point, you'll develop your relationship enough that you and the chapter brothers are ready to ask this prospective member to join. This is great news. It can be a long process to build this relationship to the point where you, the chapter and the prospect would be comfortable asking for a lifetime commitment to/from everyone involved. The Ask, which is discussed later in this book, is a delicate matter and must be handled with care.

PRE-CLOSE

Welcome to a world of 100% bid acceptance.

We'll provide you with a nice model to use when asking someone to join your organization, but first let us explain something that will make your ask 100% successful. It's called a "Pre-Close." A Pre-Close is a tactic that you can employ to guarantee that you never again offer an invitation of membership to a prospect and have that invitation declined. That's right, nobody will ever say "no" to your chapter's formal bid again.

Isn't that how it should be? An invitation to be your fraternity brother for life is something that should be handled with the utmost care. That's a big commitment you're willing to make and a really big commitment that the prospect is willing to make. Never again should you invite someone to join your organization if there is a chance they might say no. The Pre-Close solves that problem.

The Pre-Close is a simple question that, when paired with the quality responses you prepared in Step 5 (remember Feel * Felt * Found), helps you greatly increase the number of men in your chapter. Here's the question: "If we were to ask you to join the fraternity right now, would there be any reason you'd say no?"

It's a beautiful thing, that Pre-Close. Once you ask it, the prospect can either say that they're completely ready to join, or they can voice their concerns. If they voice their concerns, you turn to your Feel * Felt * Found statements and help them understand how great of an opportunity it is that you're offering.

The other amazing thing about the Pre-Close is that it allows you to recruit men all year long – even on campuses that have deferred recruitment policies. Your university may not allow you to extend bids to freshmen during certain parts of the year, but that doesn't mean you can't become their friend. Recruit year-round, but if your campus has restrictions, save the formal bid for the appropriate time of the year.

The Pre-Close is a tactic that you should employ in a separate conversation, *prior* to extending a bid to a prospect. Make sure you give the prospect plenty of time to truly come to grips with their concerns.

PRE-CLOSE

The Secret to 100% Bid Acceptance

"If we were to ask you to join the fraternity right now, would there be any reason you'd say no?"

THEY WON'T JOIN IF YOU DON'T ASK

So, now that we have that little tool in our toolbox, we'll explain how you should ask your prospects to join your fraternity.

THE FIVE STAGES OF A GREAT ASK

1. Small talk & transition
2. Ownership questions
3. Pre-close
4. Quality responses
5. Close/formal bid

Helpful Hints to Make Your Ask Successful:

✳ Do not initially approach him with more than one other member.

✳ Keep the environment comfortable for him on his terms. Do not ask him at the bar, club, or in the fraternity house.

✳ Dress appropriately. If you want to be taken seriously, dress and act the part.

✱ Practice before the meeting. Know how to answer common questions and objections by reviewing your preparations – try role-playing.

✱ Be real! This is not a cold call or sales meeting. You're about to ask one of your best friends to join your family of brothers.

✱ Compliment him on the qualities of his character that make him stand out.

✱ Keep the conversation about him.

✱ Remember, Feel * Felt * Found. Empathize. His commitment is just on the other side of his concerns. Help him get over those concerns with quality responses.

What an Ask Might Look Like:

Small Talk:

- This is simple, anytime you go to ask someone to join your organization, start with normal, friendly small talk (For reference, review the previous section, "5 F*'n Ways to Master Conversation")

Transition statement:

- *"We could talk about ____ all day, but there is something I really wanted to talk with you about."*

Ownership questions:

- *"I think the fraternity has been through a lot this year. **If you were leading a group like this, what do you think you would do?"***

- *"You are one of the best men I have ever known. I think it would be an honor for me to call you my fraternity brother someday. **What do you think?"***

- *"I think you're a strong individual with a lot of potential. A leader with character and a passion for helping others. I want you to know that I've got a lot of respect for you. Those are the same qualities our fraternity looks for in its members. **What do you think it would take for us to attract more men like yourself?"***

- *"You know the fraternity is one of the most important parts of my life, right? I've talked with the brothers and they think you're the type of person that we need as we move forward to the next level. **What do you think?**"*

Pre-close:

- *"John, if the fraternity extended you a bid for membership, what concerns might prevent you from saying yes?"*

Quality Responses

- *"I know how you feel. I felt the same way. Let me share with you what I found..."*
- *"Did I completely answer that question for you? Do you still feel like that concern would prohibit you from joining the group? Considering that, is there any other concern that would prevent you from saying yes?"*

Close/Formal Bid:

- *"John, this is a big night. The main reason I came over to see you is because I'm representing my entire fraternity to ask you an important question. We would like to formally extend to you a bid for membership to our sacred fraternity. Will you accept our proposal?"*

Great job! The Ask is the most important part of this entire step. After all, how many people have never joined because you've never asked them?

A NOTE ON PUBLIC RELATIONS

You have probably noticed that the focus of Step 6 was on interpersonal relationship building as opposed to mass marketing or building relationships with the public. You're absolutely correct in that assessment.

The Eight Steps to Limitless Possibility profess the power of personal relationships and suggest a shift away from depending on things like posters, chalking campus, rush T-shirts, mailings, events and etc. These can be very valuable in developing the image of the organization, but should not be *relied upon* for growing and developing the membership.

You can't imagine Vince Lombardi, one of the greatest coaches in football history, recruiting members for his championship teams by putting up posters and having the guys wear T-shirts that say *"Join the Packers – We get chicks!"* You can't imagine the CEO of a Fortune 500 company recruiting a top VP with chalk on the sidewalks of business schools or by holding a pig roast in the quad. So, if you want to have a top level organization, do what top level organizations do – build personal relationships.

SOME P.R. QUESTIONS TO CONSIDER

✳ If you were to create a t-shirt that expressed everything that you stand for, what would it say on it?

✳ How many members in your chapter right now joined because of printed material that they saw? Is that why you joined?

✳ What do the events that you hold to attract new members say about you? What do they say about your organization? What do they say about your brothers across the country?

✳ What three words best represent everything that your organization stands for? How could you use those on your promotional materials?

DO IT.

Experience the limitless possibilities that await your chapter right away by applying the ideas provided here:

* **Practice your skills at a social function. Again, the same skills you need to recruit a new brother are the skills you need to get a date this weekend. Go to a social function, a public area, or an event, and practice the skills taught in Step 6.**

* **Incorporate Step 6 interpersonal skills training into your membership education program. What more valuable skills could you teach your brothers than how to build positive relationships?**

* **Ask one of your alumni brothers who has a successful career in sales to come back to the chapter to provide an evening of sales skills training. You'll find out that Step 6 applies beyond your collegiate years.**

* **Identify a couple of small activities that your members enjoy doing together. Do them on the same nights every week. Use these activities as opportunities to introduce prospects to your friends and build strong relationships.**

"Good people are good because they've come to wisdom through failure. We get very little wisdom from success, you know."

~ William Saroyan~

STEP 7: GROW WISER

The pursuit of wisdom, Step 7, is the most influential, life-altering step of this eight step system. It requires the most endurance, but it yields the greatest returns.

Wisdom, as a value, has been a major part of our fraternity life. Many fraternities, like our own, challenge their members to pursue wisdom for the greater good of mankind. It is a value we share as an interfraternal community. And it is at the heart of Step 7.

But, what does wisdom have to do with recruitment? Great question.

There is this fraternity we know that has existed for more than 140 years. Their founders were brilliant gentlemen who were the epitome of what a great man should be. It was 140 years ago that this fraternity was founded, and it was about 140 years ago that this fraternity created its traditions, habits, and patterns of recruitment behavior. They built their recruitment system about 140 years ago, and with only slight changes, it has stayed the same ever since.

So, here we are now, 140 years later, and we've got this fraternity that has existed pretty well for all that time. They've built chapters all over the country and they have a proud tradition of important alumni. They are a good organization.

Somewhere along the line, however, this fraternity reached a plateau of how much they could grow. It has been decades since that plateau was originally reached and, since that time, they've maintained a constant state of goodness, not greatness, just goodness

Is this 140-year-old fraternity doing things wrong?

More importantly, could it be doing things better?

What's missing?

What's missing, according to this eight step system, is *wisdom*. This fraternity, while it has been successful, never looked beyond its own traditions, habits and patterns of behavior for new ways to grow. They never sought out a book on fraternity recruitment, for example. They also never brought in assistance from outside their fraternal walls. They believed that their founders knew best and they should just keep doing what they'd always done.

As we've already learned, if you keep on doing what you've always done, you'll keep on getting what you've always gotten.

For your recruitment efforts to yield greater results, you and your chapter need to regularly seek out new recruitment wisdom. You need to learn lessons and make adjustments – just like you do when you grow wiser in your personal life.

Do you repeat your mistakes or do you learn from them and move forward?

Wisdom is attained in two ways, lessons learned through personal experience and lessons learned through the experiences of others.

"Lessons learned through personal experience" is really just a euphemism for "failure." That's right; we're promoting failure in this section of the book. Learn to see your failures in life as stepping stones to success. The more times you fail, the more you'll be prepared for success. That is a lesson learned best by experience, but we would be remiss to not mention it.

What recruitment tactics have you tried that have failed? Which recruitment tactics get only mediocre results? Are you growing wiser?

Besides using your own personal failure as a learning mechanism, you can also gain wisdom through the experience of others. By seeking wisdom from the experience of others, you minimize the mistakes you have to make personally through internalizing the best practices of those who are qualified to offer you advice.

The key is to be smart enough, and brave enough to ask for advice from the right people.

A wise man would never ask the accountant to perform surgery nor would he ask the doctor for advice on balancing his checkbook. Likewise, he does not ask his unqualified friends, family, or alumni members for advice on *effective* recruitment or fraternity management practices. He asks experts that can help him.

As you're looking to create a revolution of limitless possibility within your organization, remember that the people who tell you something is impossible are the people who gave up too soon.

The best way to get qualified advice on recruitment or personal performance is from "experts." Do this in three ways:

1. Mentoring

The advice of a professional is priceless in saving you time, money, and energy. Ask *those who know* to be your mentors. Seek out a personal fan club of qualified superstars invested in your personal and chapter success. Find other chapters on your campus or in your fraternity that are committed to limitless possibilities and mentor each other. Ask a successful business leader to serve as your chapter's "Success Advisor." Ask someone who recruits or does sales for a living to help you re-shape your chapter's business model. Make your mentor(s) a part of your daily life.

2. Reading

There is no replacement for the magic of internalized literature. This process may only be accomplished through the written word. And come to find out, there are a lot of books out there that can help a fraternity with recruitment, they just don't necessarily say "rush" on the front. We recommend reading for a minimum of 20 minutes each day (even if it's forced) from the list of Recommended Recruitment Readings on the following pages. Perhaps there is nothing more powerful than knowing that a ¼ inch thick book can bestow upon you the life's work of the world's most accomplished men. If given the opportunity to meet the world's greatest man, what would be the value of one hour of his time? What business and world leaders can you read about to pick up tips on growing a strong organization?

3. Outside Learning

Attending conferences, seminars, workshops, speaker series and continuing/outside educational programs can be one of the best ways to truly grow wiser. It really comes down to exposing yourself to as many people, ideas and opportunities as you can. Try to put yourself in positions which allow you to see how other fraternities, organizations or businesses grow and become successful, and then try to adapt those lessons for your own use. Attend your fraternity's regional and national events. Go to the non-mandatory lectures on campus. Find out about other student organizations' leadership events on campus or nearby (and don't forget to ask the people you meet how *they* recruit). Ask your student life professionals for their recommendations.

Becoming a recruiter with the necessary wisdom to get results takes a commitment to seeking out knowledge from beyond your normal circles, as well as considering how it applies to your needs. It is equally important to TEACH and USE these learned principles and techniques. The wisdom gained immediately begins to transform you and your chapter.

We have become successful business owners, consultants, and authors due mostly to the fact that we read the words of people smarter than us as often as possible. Remember, we used to be really bad at recruitment, but then we learned through our own experiences and the experiences of others that there were amazing recruitment possibilities sitting right beneath our nose – we just needed to be willing to seek out that wisdom.

WISDOM THOUGHTS

"People who don't read are no better off than those who don't know how"

Mark Twain

"I have never let my schooling interfere with my education."

Mark Twain

"You'll be the same person in five years as you are today with two exceptions: the people you associate with, and the books that you read."

Charley Jones

"When the learner is ready, the teacher will be revealed."

Lao Tzu

Try some of the books on the Recommended Recruitment Reading list found on the following pages. And don't worry, most of them come in an audio version.

RECOMMENDED RECRUITMENT READING

How to Win Friends and Influence People
Dale Carnegie

7 Habits of Highly Successful People
Stephen Covey

The Magic of Thinking Big
David Schwartz

Remember Every Name, Every Time
Benjamin Levy

The Fine Art of Small Talk
Debra Fine

The Art of Possibility
Zander & Zander

Good to Great
Jim Collins

The Four Agreements

Don Miguel Ruiz

The Sky is Not the Limit. You Are.

Bob Davies, M.S.

You Can Make It Happen

Stedman Graham

Secrets of Closing the Sale

Zig Ziglar

The Tipping Point

Malcolm Gladwell

21 Irrefutable Laws of Leadership

Maxwell & Ziglar

Think and Grow Rich

Napoleon Hill

Purple Cow

Seth Godin

DO IT.

Experience the limitless possibilities that await your chapter right away by applying the ideas provided here:

* **Give this reading list to your friends and family as holiday gift ideas. Better yet, use the library on campus.**

* **Commit 20 minutes every day to readings from the Recommended Recruitment Reading list.**

* **Ask your student life professionals or national headquarters staff about any upcoming conferences, workshops, or seminars that could improve your chapter.**

* **Make two lists. On one list, write down everything that you think your chapter could use some advice on. On the second list, write down every person that you know who is either smarter than you or has more experience than you. Finish the second list by writing down two or three famous people you admire and would like to meet. Try to match the needs on the first list to the wisdom of the people on the second list, and ask for their mentoring. Yes, ask even the famous people.**

"We are what we repeatedly do.

Excellence, then, is not an act,

but a habit."

~Aristotle~

STEP 8: REPEAT

Wash. Rinse. Repeat. It really is good advice.

Sometimes you need to do things more than once for them to be truly effective. Imagine if you had shampooed your hair once upon a time, but then never bothered to do it again. Shampoo only works because you keep doing it over and over until it is a part of your daily routine.

The same goes for these eight steps. They only produce results if you take them beyond these pages and put them into practice. And they only create a revolution of recruitment success in your chapter if you build them into a repeatable system that becomes part of the chapter's culture. Step 8 is about taking each of the steps, doing the little things that it takes to make change, and then making that the chapter's unique growth system. A system that gets repeated year after year, semester after semester, week after week, and day after day.

Step 8 is where you transform from learner into teacher. This information should be shared with as many people as you can find within the next 48 hours. The sooner you talk about the ideas you've learned in this book, the sooner your limitless results begin to materialize.

Be mindful that this program is designed to improve the quality and quantity of your chapter to the degree of your choosing. When the lessons, exercises, and overall program are practiced daily, you will see a transformation. The work you are putting in will suddenly seem second nature – no more difficult than finding the cafeteria, tying your shoes, or singing your favorite song. How is this possible?

You are experiencing a change in your habits or *patterns of behavior*. Those things that once took full concentration to accomplish are now becoming routine activities.

Remember when you first learned how to drive a car? The first few times required determined focus as you surveyed the road, double checked instruments, and carefully evaluated every decision you were about to make with two hands firmly gripping the wheel at 10 o'clock and 2 o'clock. Fast forward just three months and you have the radio blasting, a cell phone in one hand, and you're driving with your knee while eating a Big Mac™.

You should feel excited as you realize the same transformation is about to happen to your chapter's recruitment process and, subsequently, to your chapter's potential for greatness. Where you once sat helpless, waiting for the next semester's rush you now stand empowered and ready to triple your productivity at any time of the year.

Step 8 simply suggests that the key to making this whole thing work is to make it a part of your chapter's system, re-think your chapter's business model, and include these eight steps in the new draft.

We believe that there is an exciting world waiting out there for you and your fraternity chapters, with exciting realities. Large, prosperous chapters full of involved and dedicated gentlemen, working to better the lives of each other and the communities that surround them are within reach. Your chapter can quickly become the most influential force on your campus and in your community. All it takes is the right mindset and a great plan – we have the plan, do you have the mindset?

A "great plan," however, means that attracting the best men on your campus takes more than a box of chalk, a stack of fliers, or an expensive tab for Buffalo wings. Instead consider treating your chapter like a Fortune 500 Fraternity. It is highly unlikely that Bill Gates would search for Microsoft®'s next top Vice President by posting an ad in *USA Today* for free pizza at his place or have his employees wear clever T-shirts displaying exposed women and alcohol slogans. As ridiculous as that sounds, many campuses have seen these embarrassing attempts by fraternities to attract their best leaders in a similar manner.

Take McDonald's™ for example. This is a company that started small (just like your fraternity did), but grew to be one of the most influential corporations in history. Though their advertising has always been top notch, anyone will tell you that McDonald's true success came from a simple business plan. Any McDonald's you visit for a hamburger and milkshake looks just like most other McDonald's that you've visited. McDonald's put a plan in place. It was a plan that was simple, repeatable, and offered *anyone* the opportunity to start a franchise of their own and succeed (as long as they followed the business plan). Now, McDonald's is everywhere, and probably every single fraternity brother you have shares with you the incredible possibility of a Happy Meal™ and a Coke® just by going down the block to visit their neighborhood Ronald McDonald™.

Every great business and organization talks about the same key ingredients – having the right people and executing the right plan. Fraternity chapters are no different. You have a great team of brothers to start the process. The Eight Steps to Limitless Possibility provides you with the framework for making your chapter's system (business plan) for recruitment and long-term success. This is the system that can make your chapter the most influential, successful, and exciting group of young men your campus has ever seen.

ROUND TABLE

To effectively implement this new model for limitless possibility, there's a good chance you're going to need some help. Many fraternities we have worked with in the past have gotten too caught up in leadership positions, titles, policies and committees -- especially when it comes to recruitment. These chapters are so used to putting all of the responsibility on the Recruitment Chairman's shoulders that they don't know any other way of doing things. Creating a Round Table solves that problem.

A Round Table is simple. Get like-minded people together to meet regularly and work together toward your new possibilities. For instance, if you and two other people like the ideas presented in this book, get together for a weekly meeting and start your own revolution. You don't need your whole chapter on board in order to get things started. Remember Margaret Mead's statement, "Never doubt that a small group of thoughtful people could change the world. Indeed, it's the only thing that ever has."

We know that Pareto's Principle holds true in most organizations and that 20% of the members produce 80% of the results. This Round Table idea is intended for those members who fit into the 20% category of your chapter, those 20% that are willing to hold up their end of the bargain.

Now, maybe your organization is an exception in that more than 20% are ready to rock and roll. If so, you're way ahead of the game. If not, then the others better hop on board quickly because GREATNESS doesn't wait around for mediocrity!

Purpose of the Round Table:

* Mentor the general chapter members with ongoing support and continually try to get their commitment to be a part of the round table.

* Constantly promote and teach The Eight Steps to Limitless Possibility to all members.

* Hold each other accountable to the eight step system, getting names ON the list, getting names OFF the list, and ongoing education.

* Most importantly, continue to build the organization's dream!

We've even developed an agenda for you to use during your first (and every) Round Table meeting. These eight questions will guide your Round Table meetings.

---

8 ROUND TABLE QUESTIONS

1. What percentage of time is our organization spending on the basics (People and Purpose)? How can we improve that percentage of time?

2. How have you lived the organization's purpose this week (A.C.E. your values)?

3. What did you do this week to feed your WILD DREAM for the fraternity?

4. Where will you meet your 5 new people tomorrow?

5. How has this organization enhanced your life this week?

6. Who are your 5 new prospects today?

7. What have you read/learned lately that could help the organization?

8. When and where are we meeting next?

DO IT.

Experience the limitless possibilities that await your chapter right away by applying the ideas provided here:

✳ **Organize your Round Table. If you notice a few other guys who also seem interested in a recruiting revolution for your chapter, ask them to read this book and then to join you for informal Round Table meetings once a week. Use the 8 Round Table Questions to guide your meeting.**

✳ **Use The Eight Steps to guide a new member education program. Plug in your own chapter and campus details, and see how quickly a curriculum to truly prepare brothers is born out of The Eight Steps. Better yet, build a whole membership education program that lasts until your members graduate – and even beyond.**

✳ **Use The Eight Steps to guide your chapter's strategic planning for the next year.**

✳ **Let this book do the work for you. Ask two of your brothers to read it. Watch them get excited.**

WHO DOES ALL THIS?

You may be thinking to yourself that, *"All this information is really nice, and seems like a good idea, but isn't it all supposed to be the job of the Recruitment Chairman? Isn't this just making the Recruitment Chairman's job harder?"*

Fair questions. To put it plainly, however, the answers are NO and NO. This eight step system is NOT just for the Recruitment Chairman of your chapter. Furthermore, this eight step system actually makes the job of Recruitment Chairman easier.

The only way to make this system really work requires at least a small group of your chapter members committed to changing your current system. The Recruitment Chairman can then become the "manager" of the process. It should NOT be the recruitment chairman's job to meet everyone going on the Names List. Your results won't be that great if you take that approach with this new process. The Recruitment Chairman should take the lead in managing all the members of the chapter (or at least The Round Table) and ensuring that they are doing their simple, daily habits that will lead to your chapter's success.

Your Recruitment Chairman can guide your members through all the activities in this book. It should be the Recruitment Chairman's job to ensure that *recruitment* efforts are at the top of the chapter's priority list.

This book outlines patterns of behavior that *each* member of your chapter can adopt. If you want greater results, you must do greater things than you're currently doing. Challenge your chapter to redefine the role of Recruitment Chairman and to redefine the role each brother plays in the year round recruitment process.

THE EIGHT STEPS
IN REVIEW

The Eight Steps to Limitless Possibility provides a framework for your fraternity's recruitment revolution. Follow the tips listed in this book, ask yourself the tough questions, and make The Eight Steps your chapter's system of operation.

Step 1 reminds you to focus your energy on the two basic fundamentals of your organization: People and Purpose. Get a lot of high quality brothers and make sure everyone is dedicated to your chapter's purpose.

Step 2 promotes Achieving, Communicating, and Expecting your fraternity's values in everything that you do as an organization. If you skip Step 2, you're just another boys club causing trouble for the rest of us.

Step 3 pushes you to build your chapter's dream. Get your brothers to build a recruitment dream that is so big that they will do whatever it takes – everyday – to make it a reality. The motivation to do the small things right is based on building a big enough dream.

Step 4 stretches your understanding of your potential audience and helps you understand where you can find the thousands of future brothers that are sitting out there waiting to be asked.

Step 5 implores you to know your product before you go out and try to sell it. Understand and be able to communicate the value and benefits of your organization, so that when the opportunity arises, you can sell anyone on how great it is to be in your fraternity.

Step 6 builds your interpersonal skills so that you can be confident going out into the world, shaking hands, developing friendships, and recruiting brothers.

Step 7 teaches you that to improve you must be willing to learn the lessons that make you wiser. Recruitment results will stay the same unless you continually seek out new ideas, new strategies, and new systems to take your chapter from mediocre performance to amazing results.

Step 8 instructs you to repeatedly do the little things to unearth big results. Build a new system for your chapter in which each member is taught and re-taught each component of The Eight Steps. This system ensures success for not just this semester, but for years and years to come.

Each step is necessary. They depend upon each other. Do them all and watch your results grow exponentially.

THE EIGHT STEPS TO LIMITLESS POSSIBILITY

1. **Know the Basics**

2. **A.C.E. your Values**   **How Come?**

3. **Get Motivated**

4. **Know your Audience**

5. **Know your Product**   **How To?**

6. **Develop Skills**

7. **Grow Wiser**

8. **Repeat**   **How Long?**

FREQUENTLY ASKED QUESTIONS

Often, people who talk with us about The Eight Steps to Limitless Possibility ask certain questions over and over again. Here are the most common questions we've been asked, along with some quick answers. These might help as you start to share these ideas with others in your chapter or on your campus.

Question: Where do I start?
Answer: What can you do in the next 24 hours that makes a difference? The process starts with baby steps. Start with small changes and the big ones will follow. We recommend beginning by dream building, assembling your round table, teaching others this recruitment system, and creating your Names List.

Question: What if I don't want a big chapter?
Answer: Quantity drives Quality. It doesn't matter if you want to grow 40 times larger or stay the same size. Your chapter benefits from simply having more men from which to choose.

Question: How can I ever get my guys to do any of this?
Answer: Leave the door open for all, but get started with just a few. What impact could your top five men have if they each recruited five men like themselves? The Round Table concept works great for a practical answer to this question.

Question: What if our chapter needs to work on internal issues first?
Answer: Remember the basics. People and Purpose. Save managing your mules for later. New leaders and new members will solve almost all of your problems. The answer to most fraternity problems is recruitment.

Question: I know all this already. What's the point?
Answer: To know and not to do is not to know.

Question: Where do I go for more information?
Answer: http://www.PhiredUp.com/

DO IT.

Throughout this book, we have provided suggestions for putting The Eight Steps to Limitless Possibility into action. Now is the time to do it. The change that is possible may not be incredibly easy, but it really is as simple as DOING IT. We've just provided a system that achieves results as long as you *work the system.* The choice is truly yours.

Most personal fitness trainers suggest that the hardest part of any exercise program is getting started! The same is true of this program. It takes several days or even weeks to see significant results from working out in the gym. And, even with small rewards and improvements along the way, it takes approximately 21 days for the gym to become a pattern of behavior or habit. Similarly, the hardest part of this program is just getting started and making it through the first stages of developing a pattern of behavior. The key is to build momentum, one day and one step at a time, and soon the body will feel deprived by NOT going to the gym – or, in this case, doing the things that will make your fraternity great.

THE EIGHT STEP PROCESS IS SIMPLE:

1. Understand what your fraternity is and how it works.

2. Commit to your purpose, then A.C.E. it.

3. Dream of what you could be, and let that motivate you, your chapter members, and your potential members.

4. Identify your fraternity's potential: Who do you want with you and who is available?

5. Know what you're offering, and know how to communicate it.

6. Do the little things to get who and what you want.

7. Continually grow wiser.

8. Repeat the process over and over.

Get started right now and follow this system. You'll find that the possibilities truly are limitless.

May all your dreams be achieved!

ABOUT THE AUTHORS

Matthew Mattson is the co-founder and Chief Executive Officer of Phired Up Productions, LLC. Leveraging a Master's degree in Training and Performance Improvement, and a background in public relations, collegiate admissions, fraternity expansion, human performance improvement, and nonprofit leadership education, Matt combines his passion for wisdom with a firm sense of integrity to effectively inspire thousands of organizational members toward their pinnacle of achievement.

Joshua Orendi is the co-founder and Chief Operations Officer of Phired Up Productions. Applying successful backgrounds in education, business-networking, fraternity expansion, corporate management, and executive recruitment, Josh delivers a fun but demanding style of training that empowers individuals with the belief and skill necessary to achieve limitless possibility.

Phired Up Productions provides recruitment solutions and performance improvement services uniquely designed for college fraternity men and other customers. Our integrated menu of services delivers results through three delivery methods: **Performance consulting, experiential programming, and support publications.**

Our mission is targeted especially for customers that desire a higher quantity of higher quality individuals involved in their organization – and who are interested in long-term, limitless success.

Josh Orendi and Matt Mattson founded Phired Up Productions in 2002. Since then, the team has grown to include a full spectrum of experts from many fields who all share a passion for igniting minds and improving the performance of organizational leaders.

We specialize in helping college student organizations including fraternities and sororities; service groups; cultural and religious organizations; admissions, housing and orientation groups; and other student associations.

Outside of our main collegiate market, we partner with community organizations, including business and commerce groups, charities and not-for-profits, gender and cultural issue groups, fraternal organizations, businesses, and religious institutions.

YOUR NEW RECRUITMENT PLAN

Remember:
By failing to plan, you're planning to fail

_____

_____

_____

_____

_____

_____

_____

_____

_____

_____

_____

_____

_____

_____

_____

_____